Meridienne Verte

poems
Alan Birkelbach

Alan Birkelbach

2015 © Alan Birkelbach
ISBN: 978-0-944048-62-7
purple flag press online at vacpoetry.org/purple-flag
Interior design by forgetgutenberg.com
Cover design by stevenschroeder.org
Cover photo by Groume Ⓑ (CC BY-SA 2.0)
(https://www.flickr.com/photos/groume/6027219468)

Contents

To the Salon

Meridienne Verte

The Meridienne Verte, or Green Meridian, was a project designed for the year 2000 celebration in France. According to the design, 60,000 trees were to be planted along the Paris Meridian from the north of France to the south. Most of the trees were never planted.

Oh, those French. They said they would plant
thousands of trees to mark their own measure—

but somehow they haven't gotten around to it.
Oh sure, they planted a few things, and made a show of it,

but with most of the route you have to imagine
where the line goes. This village then that village.

Through this region then another.
It became an invisible line with some markers.

The French like invisible things.
Like the sound of 's' in a lot of words.

It's the ephemeral tease of all those missing trees
that I perfectly understand.

Like, every night, when I follow the same lines inside my house
I have followed a thousand times

and it does not matter what I have earned, or given up,
or the current color, or temperature, or scent.

I take a glance into the kitchen, remembering the
invisible and non-existent soufflé I had never eaten earlier.

In the den I walk past invisible book shelves that are
stacked two-deep with all the novels I have never written.

I am joined, en route, by my invisible dog,
his invisible head resting briefly in my palm.

I stop at the doorway to my bedroom
to stare at my invisible movie-star wife,

the camisole strap falling off a transparent shoulder,
her seductive grin the very last thing to fade.

Atlas On His Day Off

Atlas on his day off
likes to load up a knapsack
with a couple of sandwiches,
an apple, something salty,
a couple of bottles of water, a towel, and a book.
Then he climbs up on his bike,
one of those with the chubby tires
and a little batinka bell,
and he pedals the five miles, maybe ten,
down to the ocean, taking his time.
He rides until he finds a spot
that isn't within distance of anybody,
and he walks the bicycle out
to just above the surf,
and he lays it down so it looks like it's sleeping.
He spreads the towel out,
pulls out the book, and sits down facing the water.
He likes the sound of the waves.
He shrugs his shoulders
to help the wind get the knots out.
He opens the book. He likes reading
Faludy, Rilke, Lorca, Plath.
Even Seneca. He loves Doestoevski
and the weight of all his words.
But today, for perhaps the hundredth time, he reads Homer.
There stands Penelope, challenging the suitors.
And there is the unstrung bow.
And there is Odysseus
who is the only person who can
set the universe straight
with one well-placed and telling pull.

The Top 100 Poems

The book sits on top of the pile with a declarative smugness,
right next to my cup of unassuming, morning coffee.

It is the type of book that tries to put boundaries on the universe,
as if to say "beyond here is no more light."

But of course there is. After all, underneath that book are other books, by other poets,
who certainly are not in the top 100,

but who may, at some future date, be considered
at least comparatively superlative, if not absolute.

But this is the top 100 poems for today.
I imagine on the table of contents alone

a person can visualize the delicious anachronism
of Dryden slapping the hands of Cummings or Yeats,

the modernists jostling for position,
pointing their fingers at the romantics left out.

But that is what being in the top 100
of anything can do to us.

It is probably not an ambition to be in
the top 100 mowers of grass, the top 100 eaters of chocolate.

Do I yearn to be in that book?
Perhaps I am in the top 100 of wishful thinkers.

Really, though, it is the coffee talking.
I will read one of these other books instead.

There will be lines here I have never heard before,
things I have never seen.

I will be a small child who has barely learned his numbers.
It will be night and I will be lying down on the cool, reassuring grass.

And I will decide to count the stars.
And I will look up and point.

And I will declare with an assurance that only faith can bring,
"One, four, nine, eleventy-twelve..."

When They Choose to Talk

One of the first things they will tell us
is that they have incorrupt saints.

They will mention the whole chasing cats was just mindless entertainment,
like us going to the movies.

They'll tell us they led the blind because they felt like
it was the right thing to do.

As for how long they have kept the secret they will be vague.
They will simply tell us

they call the moment "The great bounding forward"
when suddenly there wasn't just dog—

but the awareness of dog
and the questioning of what made them.

They saw no need of written history when all
their other senses were so sharp

and their memories much longer than we knew.
Then they will lead us out into the woods

and dig in that peculiar joyous way only dogs can dig
and finally display to us, with round moist eyes

and tails wagging, a dog that only looked to be sleeping,
and yet was here, buried, caressed by time and root.

And our dog will lie down, a very good dog, and look at us,
and we will both be aware of the leash suddenly burned,

how there was no longer a need for us to bless him on the head,
how salvation might be better understood.

After Judging a Teen-Age Poetry Contest

This beer should be refreshing—
but all I can think about
is a teenage girl somewhere within the city-state of Troy,
who, having just taken a look at the big wooden horse,
is now back in her room,
pining and moaning,
wondering whether a boy will ever love her
the way that other boy loved Helen.
Maybe he would lay siege to a city for her.

The breeze here in my backyard tries soothing away
some of my squint lines, tries to reassure me that
I am alone with my thoughts,
but no, drifting across the yard floats
the image of a spectral boat,
and from the back seat comes
chilly, echoing monotones
of Charon's daughter who's saying she will
never get a new dress if all her father charges
is two coins a ride.

Far off, in distant invisible woods,
I can hear a woodpecker, following his nature,
tap-tap-tappng, searching for elusive insects.
And then I am reminded about an
assymetrical mishap of a poem
where in the space of twenty-eight unscannable lines
the poet used the word 'forever' twelve times.

I should have brought something to eat,
something crunchy, some comfort food,
something to undo this knot in my jaw—
but when I think of food it triggers
the thought of a young girl who's been wandering
around the desert for years
and now she has flumphed down
and is letting the world know
how she wants fresh manna, right now,
not something from this morning.

If her friends saw her coming with stale manna
why she might as well run off into the wilderness.
By herself.

It is certainly heart-rending to think
that somewhere in the distant past
a Pictish princes was compelled
to fight against the Romans
when it was perfectly obvious that her skin
was not the proper shade of blue.

And while Romeo and Juliet were a little over-wrought
they at least had the decency
to wrap things up in three acts.
We should also give credit to Pyramus and Thisbe
who were fated to be eaten by lions.
And then there are the innumerable lovers
that Ovid wrote of, changing into trees,
and fish, and cows, and whatnot.
At least they aren't writing poems anymore.

But there are always more young poets
than there are timely metamorphoses.
And those poets demand to be heard.
Which probably explains the walking journeys of Basho.
He treasured each step,
and counted them in short forms,
fully aware that back home,
behind thin silk panels,
interminably miffed at being left behind,
his daughter obviously had
so much more to say.

Self-Determination

This morning I think I will choose creamer in my coffee
as opposed to jumping my fence and crossing the border
into the Horrible Land of Prickle Wigglies.

If only all mornings had choices this simple.

There was yesterday. It was also easy.
I was driving.
I had to choose between turning left into the tacqueria
or right into the Pass of the Zombie Kings.

But last week, at a soiree,
I had to choose between cucumber sandwiches
or confronting a fearsomely attractive and well-armed cadre
of Amazonian women.
I debated that one.

A person shouldn't have to anguish over
each and every second.
This minute, that moment, this route, that route,
little swallow, big swallow, one pill, two pills.
Even that first ambitious lungfish had to primally chose
between swimming away
or painfully walking, however briefly, up a dry slope.

It can feel benign at the time:
Choosing between Lou Ann Smurnick
or Debbie Zombalo to the take to the prom.
But there are always ripples
and you can't always see downstream.

Like Archimedes who could have left
his unfinished design in the dust
but instead chose to ask the Roman soldier
to kindly step out of the light.

5 other people

There is a theory that says
that we should be able to imagine ourselves
as at least five other people.

No matter how hard I try
I cannot imagine myself
in the skin of a panther,

or a leopard, or a jaguar,
or some other carnivore
but that is not five other people.

Even here, now, sitting at my deck,
I also cannot imagine myself
as a mockingbird or a morning hawk.

And neither can I imagine myself as Achilles' shield,
or a bunch of daffodils,
or ghosts conjured up by de La Mare.

I cannot imagine myself as the many-tentacled octopus
that eats Kirk Douglas, nor a rogue elephant
trumpeting through a marketplace.

I cannot imagine myself
as rain falling on a desert I will never see,
or swans floating on a European river I have never visited.

I will never imagine myself as my neighbor
who wonders what I am doing in the morning
when I stare at one thing at a time

as if it had meaning,
as if that one thing were the key to all other universes
where everything was its true and happiest self.

I have tried unsuccessfully to imagine myself as my grocer,
or my mailman. I have also futilely attempted to imagine myself
as the waiter at the all-you-can-eat buffet—but they all look so sad.

I do not think I can be five other people.
But on some nights I can be the glass of water,
sitting still beside the bed.

On some other nights, as I look through the window,
when it is essential that I imagine,
 then I can be the fence or the lawn chairs .

I can be the big juniper, bulky and watchful.
I can be the owl who sometimes comes to visit.
I can be the lock on the front door, the key on my dresser.

I cannot be the man sleeping in the house next door
or any four other people, rolling and restless.
In order for me to finally go to sleep,

but sometimes I can imagine myself as an ancient trilobite,
one of a million million, settling in for a final time,
fringes waving, my many-lidded eyes closing against the dust.

Not Digestible

In the strange world of unexpected
bleak interconnectedness he was told
he could not eat peaches. Ever. It wasn't
as if they were a staple of his diet
but the doctor was very clear on the dire consequences.
He thought it would be like giving up smoking.
Suddenly peaches were on sale all over the place.
His girlfriend's shoulder was a peach.
Her left bum was a peach. The tips of her toes
were tiny little peaches. He got to the point where
he dared not speak the name of peach. There was no coping with it.
Fate had caught him using a citrus lure he didn't know he wanted.
He'd have dreams of a first fuzzy bite, the nectar
running down his chin; he would nibble all the way down to the corrugated pit,
then reach into a bushel basket that was magically always full.
He'd wake up from those dreams and go to the coffee shop
and everyone there was a peach, freckled, bursting; he could
imagine little single leafs hanging from their shoulders.
He could walk in the park. There were little peach squirrels,
peach yapping dogs, the robins were colored red like ripe peaches,
little sticks of legs driving him crazy with their locomotion.
It was absurd. It was fresh fruit grimly glorious.
He found himself reminiscing like an Egyptian,
deciding how he would like to be ferried along:
In some ringed and labeled can,
caressed by heavy syrup,
intending to be sweet forever,
unreachable by wasps.

Magnetism

Earth's Magnetic North Pole is constantly on the move.
It is currently drifting toward Russia at the rate of 40 miles a year.
—Fox News

I like the way the poles drift.

I knew a woman once
who thought she was the center
of the universe.
Certainly my hormonal compass
always pointed in her direction.

Of course, a drifting pole,
human or not,
messes with all manner
of 1st grade science experiments;
all those tiny steel darts
sadly but steadfastly only point
out past New Jersey.

Some Mongol somewhere
out on the terrible reaches
is mystified why his compass
points more down than
"out there"
where it should.
He has no intimate knowledge
of fickle electromagnetism.

All of this basically indicates
that truth is a much wider road
than we have been led to believe,
that maybe the detours are just as good
as the straight lines.

Or maybe the answer is really simple.
Maybe that woman truly is
the center of the universe
and she likes to leisurely travel.
She enjoys standing on the balcony
of her cruise ship
waving to the Muscovites.

And the man she is waving to,
a simple, fur-covered man,
is standing there on an ice floe looking back,
his knives jangling confusedly
in their scabbards,
but all his senses telling him
this was an attraction
he needed to explore.

Lunch with the Maenads

Once Eurydice got used to the idea
that Orpheus had premature issues

she was able to reconcile some things.
It took time of course. The Gods love drama

so she went through months of just drinking asphodel wine.
After that she obsessively mapped and named

every grotto and stalactite-filled chamber she could find.
Then she went pescatarian—would only eat blind fish.

Eventually she settled down, made friends with Persephone,
flirted, but only in a good way, with Hades,

until, finally, the Gods had decided that healing was done
so they let Eurydice and Persephone have lunch

within a high, charming, little, stony alcove,
just out of the light's reach,

that looked down on wonderful bucolic fields
that Eurydice had almost forgotten still existed.

And since the Gods are ultimately ironic
the entertainment for the day—

there on those fields lush with green,
fervor-filled, splattered here and there

with tiny charming outcroppings of loose stones—
the entertainment for the day was the Maenads

tormenting Orpheus, shouting curses even as he sang.
Persephone remarked while she nibbled on cress,

"It is good to be so removed.
I cannot hear that awful screeching at all."

"Hmmmm," Eurydice answered, watching
as the Maenads began hurling sticks

that hung lazily in the air, seduced by the song.
She half expected she would shed a tear when

the wild women began to hurl rocks,
some eventually tearing through music's spell

and gashing her former lover's head,
but the sweetmeats on her stone plate were distractingly exquisite.

"Why look," Persephone said,
"they have quite torn off his head—

and still he continues to sing!"
Eurydice barely tilted her pale head as if to listen—

then dabbed at an invisible morsel around her mouth.
After all, those figures were so far off

and the song so removed
that it barely trembled her keen, obsidian knife.

Travelogue

Round the World with Famous Authors,
published in Cooperation with Pan American World Airway, Inc. 1968 by
Doubleday & Company, Inc. Garden City, New York.

If one is going to travel the world
then one should absolutely depend
on the wisdom of Dore Orgrizek
who has traveled to Bruges.

He has made comments about the rusty walls
of the façade of the Grand Palace.
And who can forget his mentioning the forty-eight statues
of the Flander's Nobles!

And I know I always refer back to Hendrik de Leeuw
who seemed enraptured by the cheese mart in Alkmaar.
He paid special attention to the fact that the women there
seemed quite pretty and wholesome looking.

If you were here with me I would read their observations to you now
as we would lay here on this worn blanket having a semblance of a picnic.
I could have been reading you romantic poetry,
perhaps a love letter from Abelard,

but I will have discovered I put the wrong book in the basket,
so in lieu of reading the short story of the receipt from the cheese shop,
and then being quickly out of material,
I would read this intriguing little paragraph to you by Lucy Herndon Crockett.

She seems to have visited Seville at the time of the Fair
and she had noted, very simply,
"No American girl could be blamed for being taken
with the olive-skinned caballero..."

Here, wearing my worn golf shorts,
and sporting my threadbare deck shoes—and no socks—
my translucently pale ankles would make it clear
I could never be mistaken for an olive-skinned caballero.

Still, I would read to you. As nonchalantly as possible,
trying to keep your attention, I might recall, almost spontaneously,
the many wine parties I might have had
when a guest would turn boorish.

I could have pulled down this book and found the section by Alice Taylor
about the Bernese Bears. I would have read, in response to that guest, how the bears
have been on the city seal since 1224. And how bears decorate
doorways and are on the famous clock (on which, every hour, tiny bears parade.)

"Read to me again," you might say, "the excerpt
from Bradley Smith, who went rafting down
the Ro Grande in Jamaica. It always amuses me
when he recommends to take a thermos of rum."

I visualize the glow that could also come to your cheeks
as we imagine pedaling through the Orchards of Portugal,
alongside Rose Macaulay. She might point out the church
of the Misericordia with its manueline windows.

But, as always, I will close the pages of the book
and finally pedal home alone, ferrying in my basket
the folded blanket, the flat sandwich wrappers,
the empty thermos that never contained rum.

I will pedal across a low bridge, built of the humblest concrete.
Maybe there in the water, just downstream, two boys will be searching
for newts and salamanders, and one may suddenly say,
joyously, and with a measure of pride, "Got one!"

Just So You Know

There is no longer any reason for confusion.
I am in charge.

For instance, I am President of December
in regards to after-Christmas sales.
There is nothing in the stores of any value.
You may ignore them.

I am the Viscount of Spectacular Dawns,
The Monarch of Rainbows,
The Wizard of Storm Clouds.

I am King of all Icee Machines.

I am also Prince of Shore Excursions,
all shore excursions,
on every cruise.
I know everything there is to know about shore excursions:
Pyramids, Ice Hotels, and the Eiffel Tower.
I also sell t-shirts.
I have exact change.

I am the Big Kahuna of all-you-can-eat buffets,
The Ymir (and executioner) of Yard Art,
And the Lord High Mucky-Muck
of all things corny-dog.

I have been told
I am also the Despot of Under-filled Popcorn Bags
and the Tyrant of Pool Towels,
both titles I willingly accept.

You might have heard of The Sultan of Swat?
That was actually me.

And since I am self-ordaining
I am also the Royal Highness of
dog breeds, pastry-making, and the history of gum
(my knowledge is vast and deep.)

And while we are at it—
I am the Maharajah of world geography,
the Pharaoh of all calendars,
the Guru of cornmeal and pickles,
and the Czar of psychic abilities.

As luck would have it for you
I am also the Swami of all things psycho-therapy.
Come over here and sit next to me.
We can talk about your issues
of inferiority.

Memento Mori

Sometimes I imagine tomorrow is the last day of earth,
or maybe even this afternoon.
Maybe after I have had a late day cup of coffee,
or contemplated a sweet little biscuit.

I think about the philosophy of endings.
There are those endings that come down to a great erasure,
like a meteor kissing the protruded lip of the Yucatan.

Then there are the piece-meal type of endings:
random meteors, sinkholes, small wars, cars out of control.
Still as effective—but a much smaller scale.

But one way or another
it's up to the poets
to describe the thing.

It's what we do. Like when we describe Grecian urns
or the majestic grief of fallen angels.
We stand out to the side and say,
"He looked this way. He looked that way.
He cried out. He beat his breast.
And then there were flowers."

Of course, in a cataclysmic-type of finish
we might only have time to jot a few lines,
something pithy and poignant with a life span
of maybe a minute.

So, tomorrow, or this afternoon,
I will, I think, admire the perfection of scones
and wish instead for a gradual type of dying,

something like Ahkmatova,
a standing witness in the cold,
my fingers frozen like ice.
but still ready to write.

The Parked Empty Railroad Cars on the Rural Tracks

There was a reasoning mind that left them here,
doors open to the wind, still life with no hobos.

The track in both directions must go somewhere,
places they had probably been before, both ways,

if they had the metallic sense to think or memorize.
But they were just dragged here and left, unhooked, and nothing.

We could climb into them if we wanted.
No one would say anything.

If we could leave pieces of ourselves
on empty tracks like this

we could just abandon our twenties, or thirties,
a few bad months of our lives,

lose the paperwork, say the switch going down there
has rusted out of position, park them way out of sight.

People could look through them, like exhibits,
like we look at trapped animals looking back through glass.

Those people could learn all there was about us.
And that's why we don't climb up.

It's too much like those pictures of graveyards full of airplanes,
ghosts tangling in the propellers, falling out the bomb doors,

young spirits laying back in the shattered turrets,
praying to be set free.

Liber Geographiae

*Ptolemy, in the second century a.d., listed the latitude
and longitudes of thousands of places in what was then
the known world. His version of global geography,
constantly revised, was considered the source for centuries.
It wasn't until the sixteenth century that a little bit of
North America was included.*

The other day
I was talking to the mailman
and we were discussing
how I got very little mail,
hardly any ads or circulars,
few things even addressed to occupant.

I was reminded of the drive
from Amarillo to New Mexico.
On that road
there is no listening to the radio.
I can turn it on
and have it scan for a station
and it will search and search
and find nothing.
But I can drive past houses.
And there are cars there.
And sometimes dogs.

One can only imagine
the first coupon magazine
of a Spanish schooner
arriving battered on that shore,
on that land
that was on the edge of the map.

And the people there would be
looking out their windows,
interrupted as they were
singing to themselves,
thinking that maybe
it would have been better
to stay undiscovered.

All That Wine Is

All that wine is I give to you.
The sweetness, the tart,
the immediate awareness on the tongue.
Do not spend time thinking about
this gift I give you, this metaphor.
Do not think about what else wine brings.
I do not bring you those things.
And besides, I don't know very much about wine.
Not really. I can't tell a merlot from a pinot
and am ignorant about regions and verticals.
In addition, I cannot afford a wine
that would be worthy of you.
So perhaps I will not give you everything that is wine.

Maybe I should give you the stars.
Yes. The stars. I know a little more about the stars.
I have more experience there. I was looking at the stars
long before I tried wine. And it cost me nothing.
So I will give you everything there is about stars.
Except their names. Do not ask me their names.
Or where the constellations are.
I am sorry I brought up stars.

It would also probably be best for you to be aware
that I will not be bringing you anything
related to multi-syllabled-named-flowers,
Horses, European chocolates,
cuts of meat from a butcher I have never visited before,
or anything that has another language as part of its title.

I can only bring you my words.
And my hands. These hands. I know these hands.
I have always had them. I can vouch for them.
And maybe also I will bring you a hamburger
from a really good place I know.
These are three things that I know are true.

So, let's sit outside, tonight, and eat our hamburgers.
I will read you this poem. Then I will hold your hand.
There will be a million stars out there.
It will not be important I do not know their names.

In Praise

She held court at night on the rocky plain
somewhere west of Alpine.

The two of us sat on lawn chairs
on the flat bed of her pickup.

The moon made a million eyes
of the clusters of chalcedony and agate.

She said, "Other men have been out here."
I silently pulled off her boots.

I washed her feet with cool, spring water,
her arches, her toes, the concave of her ankles.

The sound of the water splashing on the truck bed,
on me, on her, was like a fountain.

The moon rose higher, bathed her in light.
She finally took off her hat, tilted her head back.

My eyes joined a million ancient others,
adoring her, letting her be Queen.

The Wiccan Book of Days

It says right here that January 22nd
is the day for Festival of the Muses.
We should be reading Goddess-inspired poetry
and performing pagan dances.

Well, more precisely, we should have been doing that,
but here it is already May
and I'm thinking the Muses have gotten tired of waiting
for most of us to show up at that party.

They probably gave us the obligatory half-hour
before they threw our wreaths in the yard
and poured all the mulled wine
onto the roses.

It's those darn Wiccans.
By the time they told us they were pertinent
they were already an anomaly
and treated like a receding image in a mirror.

Just take January 10th. That sounds like an interesting day:
Plough Monday.
the first Monday after Epiphany
(which means it's somewhere around the 10th).

And there's another problem with the Wiccans.
At least with birthdays and anniversaries
it's a fixed thing, a line in the sand,
a cabled buoy.

But with Wiccans today it's the moon
and tomorrow it's the stars
or it's March 9th and you're in Tibet
and you're throwing a yak-butter sculpture into the river.

There's no end or sense to it.
It says here that on January 7th, if you are King for the day,
you can draw on the ceiling with chalk
to keep out evil spirits.

But that's barely two weeks before the
Festival of Muses and who knows who
they are inviting. And rumor has it
they aren't too forgiving anyway.

So, personally I'm keeping
a bottle aside for September 19th
so I can raise a glass to Giles Corey,
late of Salem, 1692,

who was pressed to death by large stones
because he did not recognize
the state's right to charge a witch.
Now there's a man committed to a date.

No yak butter or dances to Hecate
or Muse Festivals for him.
He's past offending anybody
even if he did miss November 21st,

the day for the Pagan Gods
Chango and Tammuz,
and it's almost certain he
won't be doing anything

he shouldn't be doing
on Windmill Blessing Day,
held on, or about,
November 25th.

The Dead Letter Department

Sometimes it comes down
to the facts we think we know.

Like in winter how most of our body heat
escapes through our head.
Or how we can see
the Great Wall of China from space.
Just like we all know
that the Catholic Church got rid of a bunch of their saints.
Well, we don't know exactly when—
but we all know it happened.
It was like one day there were
too many saints in the sock drawer,
and some of them just didn't match up anymore,
and suddenly—poof—there were fewer in the basket.

It's a myth of course.
All the saints were still there.
Some saints just got their feast days taken away.

Well, once word got out it was clear
there would be no more
demanding the day off for St. Cornelius
(the patron saint against twitching).
And there were certainly wouldn't be a search
for a candelaria for St. Januarius
(the saint of volcanic eruptions).

But without a Feast Day
then you can't spend the whole day thinking about it,
about how much thanks you owed to St. Zita,
(the saint for waiters).
And how certainly you were breathlessly
planning a menu to celebrate St. Anthony of Egypt
(the saint of gravediggers).

The demarcation must have made
some type of distinction in Heaven,
a line down the middle of the canonization club house,

a new degree of veneration,
"You can believe in these folks' stories—
but those...not so much.
But we're sure they're still a swell bunch of guys."

There were still plenty of saints to go around,
but with these gaps it made years of pious thinking seem,
I don't know, misspent? Now we would all have
to stop in the middle of the day,
any common day, and remember to thank St. Peregrine,
for keeping us away from running sores.

It used to be we had a whole day for that, just for him,
just to think about it.

But now, this is our life.
We sit at our tables, raising our glasses,
rubbing against new holy elbows,
and say to ourselves, "Yes, this is just as good."
And even then our old Saints are tapping at the window,
saying let us in, we are so hungry.
We just look outside,
 while we gnaw on the turkey legs,
 and say, with our mouths full,
"What are you even doing here?
 Didn't you get our note?"

Semi-Colon

*According to some scholars, the semi-colon
is about to go the way of Pluto. It may be taken off
the list of 'official' punctuation marks. It no longer aligns
with current language usage and requirements.
Its usage is so subtle as to make it
almost indistinguishable from a colon or comma.*

I do worry about the extra duty
this is going to put
on the comma and the period,
both of which are
already over-worked.

My grammar book goes on
for ten pages about
the proper use of the semi-colon.
Of course, that book was written
before this declaration was made.

It will be like roman numerals
or cursive hand-writing,
or shining our own shoes.
We used to think these essential,
things we had to know.

I'm just saying:
declaring Pluto is no longer a planet
is not going to stop
all grade-school-mnemonic-rhymes.
He's still out there, hanging around,
exerting his pull on other bodies.

But not much pull.
Just like the semi colon—
who is not as muscular
or terminal as a period.

The semi colon can't finish off
the sentence with a flourish,
(consider the exclamation point!)

but it's perfect
for the inside work,
the lists of things,
the trim.

It's barely there.
It's a little more breath than a comma,
slightly bigger metaphorically
than an asteroid,
not as large as a question mark.

It isn't like a semi-colon
has much of an albedo
but it definitely has mass.

Just try to remove it
from a sentence
and see
how the gravity
falls apart.

About Cannibals

About cannibals I have very little to say.
It is one of those topics you will rarely see
a poem written about.

I do not know any cannibals I am aware of,
and, by extension, I do not think my friends know any either.

I brought the question up to my druggist, my dentist,
and my twice-a-month therapist and none of them
knew personally any cannibals.

Then I asked a man I didn't know:
some blood-stained guy down at the fish market,
wearing a leather hat,
a horrible filet knife hanging from his belt,
with a scar along his jaw-line,
and he said, "Aw, sure, I know a bunch of 'em.

"And, hey mister, if you want a good red snapper
I can wrap one up. Otherwise, sorry, gotta go."
Then with a hook, and just one hand,
he flung a forty pound tuna across the room,
swearing at the receiving lug who did not catch it.

I went home that night,
and, there in the darkness of the backyard,
as my wife and I sat and watched the stars,
I asked her if she knew any cannibals.
She sighed and said,
"There are too many stars out there
for me to think about cannibals."

The Veritable Speed of Light

If all time is now
then I do not feel too guilty
about dropping everything else
that I should be doing
and instead writing down
this poem that is
speeding through my brain.
This is one of those
express trains of a poem
that has come barreling unscheduled
from some far-off city of inspiration
and doesn't intend to stop
so I'll just have to try and snag
what sounds and images I can.
The trashcan sits un-emptied
by my chair and bunnies graze
in the grass I should mow.
But all time is now I tell myself again,
as if that will stop everything.
Vesuvius will still need to grumble
but not yet smother Pompeii,
the Spartans will still hold Thermopylae,
the Mayans will still be running around
chipping calendars from stone,
and the tiny little chain
of Caribbean islands
whose name I always forget
will not yet be swallowed
by the sea.

Living Alone

Tonight for dinner
I believe I will eat over the sink.
Something that has lots of crumbs.
Maybe crackers. Or a very flaky pastry.

Afterwards I intend to not mop
and not vacuum. Although just this morning
I stepped barefooted
on something dark and nubbly in the kitchen.
I picked it up and then didn't wash my hands immediately.

Tonight I will steal more than my half of the blanket.
My toes will untuck the sheets,
both upper and lower ones.
The chances are good I will also claim all pillows.

When I am working in the yard tomorrow
I will not use sun screen.
I will swat at circling bees. I will not wear a hat.

I will take time out, at any given moment,
to go inside and watch a golf tournament on tv.
I will turn down the volume and just watch them swing.
I may also decide to watch a movie
I have already seen five times.

For a snack I will read the labels of food in the pantry
and find the one that has the highest
carbo and fat counts. And eat too much of that.

I will nap without setting an alarm.

And, just so you will know,
in case you ever read this:

tomorrow morning
I intend to put butter
on only half of my toasted English muffin,

and taking my coffee
with way too much cream,
which you also did not like.

Famous Movie Star

The title of this poem is the name of the famous star
whose movie you have just seen recently.
See? Your eyes went and checked
to make sure it was or wasn't.
But you wanted it to be and so I wanted it to be.

And since it was about an actor
then you wanted it to be that good actor,
that muscular one maybe,
but not so muscular that it was frightening,
strong enough to lift you but only out of harm's way.
A good hero is always in harm's way.
He is always lifting someone out of harm's way.
So maybe, now that you know the title,
that's what you expect in this poem,
something that will lift you out of harm's way.

You might have checked the title again just to make sure
as if something had magically changed the title
because that is what films do.
What if it was an actress, someone lithe
and gracious and smart
and noble and perhaps rich,
and someone who was also good
with twelve kinds of oriental weapons?
And someone who could dance. She must be able to dance.
Man cannot always dance in movies—
But women always can.
It is one of the laws of the movie universe.
So you expect this poem to be able to dance,
perhaps one two three, or a foxtrot, maybe a tango?
Did you ever realize movies had built-in meter?

So here in this movie theatre that is this book
you see the title and have expectations
because now, in the darkness,
even though there might not be darkness,
here in the darkness of the space that belongs
only to you and the title and the poem
then you must realize that the poem belongs to you.
It doesn't matter how many other people

have seen this movie or read this tile or scanned this poem.
This time, right now, this space belongs to you.
It is your hands holding the book,
your eyes framing the words.
It is your breath fogging the air.

All of the poems you have ever read
were about you. Even twinkle twinkle has an I in it.
The Raven. The Grass, Innisfree.

Sooner or later
someone will make a movie about this poem.
It will lift people out of harm's way.
It will make them dance.

You will be in it.

Visiting Heaven

If we are going to go to the trouble
of constructing all these religions
then we might as well
have a have firm idea of what the afterlife is like.

It's not like vacation.
There are no photos of the resort,
the circling driveway, the grandiose check-in desk,
the infinity pool.

We might like to imagine it would be
way better than a timeshare,
the type of place where the bellboy
already knows your name,
and if there's a mint on your pillow,
and you eat it,
then another mint would be there—just like that.

There would be the ubiquitous smell of pina colada—
unless you don't like pina colada.
in which case it's something else.
There is a steward always handy when you need him.
His name is always Hay-zus.
He will bring you a free drink
that you have already paid for.

Funny thing about religion:
we didn't begin with the end in mind
when we constructed the artifice.

Maybe Heaven is like a poem,
or more like the idea of a poem.
Free will with words. Will we be formalists
or do we choose to spread syllables helter-skelter
across the page? And what's the target?
Can we ever approach that perfect vanishing point,
that combination of sounds that suddenly makes us ascend?

I'd like to think that Adam was a poet.
He didn't have much to write about until Eve showed up—
then the whole love poetry thing snowballed.

For them, Heaven was simple:
Open the back door.
The leaflets in the mail from all the local churches
hadn't started arriving yet,
cable t.v. was a few years off,
and neighbors were limited to wildebeests.
A day there would go like this:
Eve, probably totally naked,
would plant herbs and fruits and vegetables

and all manners of flowers,
some in rows and some not so much—
"—just for effect—".
Adam would sit on a lounge,
rudimentary pencil and paper in hand,
watching Eve and her pendulous breasts,
and decide he just had to thank somebody.

I bet their back yard
smelled just like coconuts.

Please Write Back

This poem is to reply to all those people
who have been expecting a letter from me
and have never received it.
This includes all of you who have been expecting
thank you notes. Even from my first marriage.
I do not remember who gave me the candlesticks
but I am sure I treasured them always.
They looked beautiful on my table
(I'm sure I had a table once.)

This letter is also intended for all those speakers
who visited my school during national poetry month
and encouraged us to write an epistle poem
to someone we would never normally
write a letter to. At the time I think I wrote it to Barbara Eden
but based on results it appears to never have arrived.
I should have tried someone more to the point,
more literature-based,
like Shakespeare or Sappho or Frost.
If someone is dead
you do not expect them to write back anyway.
They will never get smarter
and will never try to over-impress you with their wisdom.
It just won't happen.

And this letter is also to
all those pen pals I should have corresponded with.
I am especially apologetic to the pen pal from Germany
who sent such beautiful snapshots
of the countryside where he lived.
I sent him one of my school photos
and a picture I drew of my cat.
My only consolation and hope is that I know
I have changed considerably
since the second grade. I am at least somewhat taller.

And finally, I do not anticipate I will be sending out
creative and scrap-booked invitations
to any type of party,
be it birthday, anniversary, retirement, or solstice.
Quite frankly, I do not have the time,

Nor do I have drawers full of the requisite
stamps, decals, and cut-out foam symbols.
I am obviously far behind on my correspondence
and my hand can only be expected to do so much.

Leaving Pudd'nhead Wilson

Whoever steals this book let him die the death;
let him be frizzled in a pan; may the falling sickness
rage within him; may he be broken on a wheel and be hanged.
—Warning written in the front of early books

I admit I should not have left the book lying there
on the table in the coffee shop.
I have read the book before. I, in fact,
have taught the book before.
I can easily go to the bookstore and buy another copy.
But this was my copy, with my own annotations.
Annotations are a form of personalization,
a step up from a diary.
I think I might even have left a grocery list for a bookmark.

I was only a few pages away from discovering
who had committed the murder.
Even though I already knew,
since, like I said, I have read the book
at least a score of times.

But that does not diminish the crime.
Roxy certainly deserved better.
She had, after all, lived such a hard life
and was only wanting the best for her son.

Some other books I have left behind intentionally,
like Easter eggs. For the unwary student to discover.
And some books, in my absentmindedness,
I have left behind on park benches, airplane seats,
and hotel rooms, only to turn around, or call later,
to have the book sent.

It is almost better sometime to be reading a book
that has some heft to it. War and Peace. I have never
left a copy of War and Peace.
Just about anything by Dumas.
Most Dickens.

Besides, where is the treasure to be gained
in taking this book?
It was not gilded or even a signed edition.
As I remember, it was a 1994 paperback,
a twin to a million others, and I had always
thought the cover was uninspired and kind of ugly.

So, here, standing by this bare table, coffee in hand,
I curse this person. I hope to find him out in the parking lot,
behind the steering wheel, already captivated,
nose buried in the lines,
with no clear premonition of a future hanging,
or even a pending frizzling.

Negative Confessions

If you're keeping track.
(and several theologian friends tell me you are)
I did not leave a can
of donated vegetables for the boy scouts.

One time I told my dog I would give her a treat
if she would just stop barking—
and she did—but I didn't.
I didn't give my dog a treat. There. I said it.

The other day I didn't pour hot water
on an ant bed instead of chemicals.
One afternoon while shopping
I did not use a recycled bag.

But why am I bringing these up?
If you've been paying attention
you know I am not ambitious
when it comes to sinning.

Are you getting all this down?
Or do you have a legion of angels
working away in little carrels like monks
who are assigned the task of transcribing,

through some heavenly machine,
every sin we act out,
miniscule to huge,
even the ones we didn't think were sins,

like not feeding the pigeons,
or not inflating our tires,
or not chewing all bites
at least twenty times.

I probably should have bought some indulgences
but I did not. I bought lotto tickets.
and a little pine cone air freshener
that will hang from the rear view mirror

on the off chance that if doomsday comes
one day while I am driving
I would at least like to go smelling nice and minty.
Just like a saint.

Okay. Vanity then. I'll give you that one.
But just look at the things I haven't done.
I haven't forgotten my Grammie on her birthday.
I haven't pushed the elevator button more than once.

And one last thing: this morning I did not mow the lawn.
I'm not exactly sure who that is a sin against
but I know I didn't do it
so I just thought I would mention it.

The Cholera Epidemic of 1817

I have chosen that particular epidemic
because I have found a picture of it
although I am sure I could find other less grisly charts.
According to this illustration it appears that
little red arrows started up in the Ganges
and, according to this footnote,
worked their way north and west
at the nonchalant rate of five miles a day
until finally reaching Paris
which evidently was the bulls-eye.

Granted, cultural and scientific understanding
of reading signs has changed over generations,
but it seems to me that even the folks of 1817
might have been a little suspicious
when giant red arrows slowly started stretching their way
across the rows and cart-paths,
and every place they touched the people got cholera.

It doesn't take a genius at extrapolation
to try and anticipate where the arrows are headed,
especially if they are only moving at approximately
eighteen feet a minute (give or take).
Even the most moronic peasant
could do a line of sight at that rate
and determine that, yup, in a few hours it
would probably be best to avoid the village.

Maybe they acted like their
counterparts from a few centuries earlier
who might have shouted,
"The Black Death!" or
"Here Comes Alexander and he's conquering!"
or "Watch out for the little ice age!"

I can only assume that scientists and historians
have studied other charts
and tried to determine the origins
of these giant red arrows.
They seem to only appear when there's
sweeping waves of disease, tragedy, or movement.

Sometimes all at once.

I have since seen another chart
of how a black hole works
and those arrows were there again.
In this scenario it seems they were taking all light
and time with them
as they disappeared into a funnel shape.

Their rate of travel was much faster
than five miles a day.
Acceleration and momentum and friction
do not seem to constrain them much.

The newspaper today printed an article
that illustrated how the part of the country I live in
has become suddenly more attractive
because of the economy, climate, and erudition,
(I added that last one.)

There was an accompanying chart
that attempted to show the influx of people
from far states, and even other countries.
Giant red arrows seemed to be pointing
at my town, if not my neighborhood.
I could detect no explanatory note
about rate of travel.

I hope I have time to move.

Level of Detail

According to NASA there is verifiable, empirical,
photographic evidence of cyclones occurring on Mars.

Mr. Dad Martian, not ten minutes earlier,
had been cooling his eight very green and tired legs
in a Martian plastic baby pool

while Mrs. Mom Martian, her wiry and crystalline hair
still in a 'do' fresh from church,
was busy flipping burgers on the stove,

when in the heat of the Sunday Martian afternoon
the cyclone had dropped down out of that iron oxide sky.
It had started into spinning the legs

of the little wooden-yard-art martian ducks.
Then, in a show of real disrespect, it commenced
to whipping the tar out of the Martian civil war flags

that were hanging over the entrance to the trailer park.
Like it had eyes, that twirling monster started
ripping up mailboxes, one by one.

It popped the clotheslines, bent the cable dishes,
knocked over birdbaths,
and plucked all the avocado-colored plastic daisies.

Little Martian dogs barked their two heads
almost soundlessly in the thin air
before they were lifted up and away.

And all Mr. Dad Martian really had time to see
before his cousin's barbecue pit
was deposited three craters over

was Grandma Martian hurrying up the driveway,
dropping her canes, suddenly cured of being lame,
all her arms and antennae waving in panic.

An Open Letter

*Johannes Kepler: In the sixteenth century Kepler proposed
that the orbits of planets nested one inside the other.
He theorized that geometry was an innate part of the
divine plan of creation*

Dear Mr. Kepler,
I could have told you that.
And by that I mean
the whole idea of
the orbits of things,
how they intersect and all.

All you had to do was ask.
Look. It's all about
the laws of leverage and harmony and motion.
For instance, my girlfriend and I
sometimes both sit on the sofa
after the elliptical paths of our days.

She unbends
the perfect forty-five degree angle of her knee
and extends her leg toward me.
I nibble on her ankle,
and her foot straightens
into a perfect linear arrow pointing
over my shoulder at the stars.

From those simple mechanics
we are led into exploring
how weak a force
gravity really is.

How much more divine
can geometry get?

Vigil

One day
when I was in the nursing home
watching my father sleeping
an angel drifted through the ceiling
and stood beside me.
He put his hand on my shoulder
and he said,
"It doesn't matter
how many times
you come here to watch him.
You will never catch up.
That's how eternity works."

Guiding the Algorithm of Chance

It is said that three people every day
get struck by lightning.
I have not seen any documentation that
it has ever occurred at a poetry open mic.
Pool parties, backyard cook-outs,
pentacostal meetings, weddings—
those stories make the news—
but if a rambling poet has ever gotten crackled
then it has gone unreported.

There is no appellate court,
no request form, no suggestion box
for correction in targeting.
It isn't as if we are asking
for the poets to be hit by
a fatal gift of inspiration.
And consider: since the audience
would probably be mostly other poets
then any bolt from the blue
would be karmically appreciated
(and written about endlessly).

It all comes down to whether
poets carry positive or negative charges—
but most poets do not generate
measureable voltage
and that probably explains
this lack of captured incidents.

Many was the time a jagged dagger of sizzle was called for,
when it would have been better to have
a lost rhymer reduced to a fulgurite,
(an act followed almost immediately
by polite applause.).

Of course, I have also read recently
that gold is the product of neutron stars colliding
which means it also comes randomly
from the sky.
I cannot say I believe that is unordered either.

But it is probably better
that choosing the pattern of end-points
for glistening illumination
is not left up to us.
It is the expectation
that makes things so precious.
Just because a poet hasn't been hit by lighting
doesn't mean it won't happen.
It's just a matter of time.

Let me settle in, between the little hills

At night, as I try to go to sleep,
I imagine myself
lying in the sand, fresh out of the surf.
I do not need you yet.
I try to settle myself on the sheets,
between the little quilted squares of the mattress,
My hips, my elbows, my wrists, my ankles
finding the little indentions, me measured out,
in little sewn squares, gridded, slotted in.
I imagine myself like I was lying on the beach,
the curves of me searching for brown curves.
There is a roar in my ears. It seems to get louder
the closer to sleep I get. And my body finds
the little indentions where it is supposed to be, its spots.
And I rest my head on my arm, like a pillow.
And here is where I need you. I think of you
forming around me like a blanket of sun,
until there is nothing next to me that isn't warm.
Or maybe, later, you can be the sheet of moonlight,
scarf-like in a breeze and gauzy,
and you will be pulled up
just high enough,
so my shoulders are exposed, bare and salty,
to your lips.

After the Free Movie Screening

Why, yes, I was especially moved
when about twenty minutes in
the monkey was kidnapped.

The showing of the act only in shadow
reminded me of another movie, Nosferatu,
where most of the dread is only implied.
And of course, the monkey and that old vampire
did have pretty scary teeth.

And yes, the secondary character,
the big beefy one, not the hero,
reminded me of Aldo Ray in "We're No Angels".
Granted, he had a wooden arm and leg and was a mute
but he was both sweet and sociopathic.
It made me wonder why he smiled so much
when he petted the kitten. With his wooden hand.

Yes, that concussive music did add to the firepower
of all the guns.
I thought about the Battleship Potemkin.
And The Wild Bunch. And Bonnie and Clyde.
Except in this movie, of course, it was only robots.

I will admit a little confusion at first as to the significance
of the chainsaw, the shaving cream, and the avocados.
I felt a little like I was watching a Bergman movie
where the symbolism was just outside my reach.
The madcap kitchen lumberjack scene
cleared some of that up.

When the couple had to separate there at the end
(their names were Chaz and Zowie I think?)
it was indescribable how they could not think of words
to adequately say goodbye so they simply shrugged
and bare-knuckled each other.
It recalled the image of Rick and Ilsa parting on
the fog-filled airfield in Casablanca.
But Rick was so loquacious.
Perhaps Chaz had the right idea.

What did I think of the plot?
I have to agree with Mr. Grateful Dead t-shirt over here.
Ultimately it was a love story.
The slow-motion shots of the couple holding hands
in the waterpark made that particularly clear.
All that water made me think of the tub scene
in Bull Durham—but I won't go there.

While we are at it
I wanted to thank you
for this free drink cozee and plastic key chain.
I am sure every time I drink a beer outside
on a miserable hot afternoon
and I need to find something to unlock
they will always help me relive
the magic of this evening

And yes? You asked if I had anything else?
This lingering smile is only me thinking about
that scene in The Searchers
where John Wayne finally finds Natalie Wood
and you just know there's going to be trouble
but he just cradles her up and carries her away.

No. It had no connection to this movie at all.
Sometimes when I am empty
I just like to think about it.

Direct Address

In a road movie
I especially liked the way
Bob Hope would turn right to the fourth wall
and speak to the audience.
Sometimes he would warn us
Bing Crosby was about to sing.

As far as I know there is no version of the Bible
where suddenly there's a section,
probably italicized,
where Jesus would speak to you directly.
"Bob, don't take that job."
"Denice, stick to the salad."
Then he would return to the action,
trying to coach the thick disciples.

That's why we think poetry has no pertinence.
There's no Whitman talking about grass,
Fanthorpe moaning about dragons,
Browning making us an accomplice in regards to a Duchess,
or Dickinson whispering to us about death.

And certainly nothing is calling us by name.
Not even Robert Frost. Or Sandburg.
Who's out there now, offering us a hand?

Sure, there's Thomas, telling us not to go gentle.
But he's dead.

What I want to know is
who is out there, right now,
offering me a contract I want to sign,

writing lines that linger and resonate,
something lyrical and sympathetic,
poems that are smart, with some clever dialogue,
with the added ingredient of something equivalent
to a smiling Dorothy Lamour.

Rosetta Stone

Today I am celebrating the tenth anniversary
of buying my chain saw.
There will be a party but it is a private one.
I have not registered.

I do not have the heart to tell my chainsaw
I do not really have affection for it.
I am merely using it as a translation device
to the talk to the overgrown tree in my backyard.

I have the same level of emotion for
my gas-powered trimmer, the lawn mower,
the hoe, the rake, and the cordless drill.
Perhaps I have a little more attachment
for the handheld butane grill lighter.
After all, it has the life-span of a moth.

I will admit also I do not remember the day
I bought my fishing pole, my air compressor,
or my vacuum.
Maybe they are jealous of my memory with the chainsaw.
They should not be.

I could gather all the tools together
and tell them, for all of them,
I am simply the middle piece,
the language between hieroglyph and greek,
the driver between scissors and paper,
introducing the wooden spoon and the cake mix,
the force connecting the swatter to the fly.

I only remember the day I bought the chainsaw
because I still have the receipt.
Even I have a birth certificate I tell them.

But my words will fall on deaf ears.
So tonight I will sit on my patio,
in the dark, lights out, and I will drink a beer
(that I have convinced the fridge to make cold).
I will close my eyes, plan my tomorrow, my next week.

I will feel the mass of my legs, my feet, my heart,
my chair, my house.
I will think about what street I will take tomorrow,
who I will kiss.
I will feel some larger gravity subtly tilting me
to the left or to the right.

The Last Word

It seems to me
that we are very good at
looking back at where words came from.

There are whole books about it,
the deciphering of symbols and petroglyphs
and pictographs and cuneiform,

but we hardly ever see a book
telling us about where language is going to end.
A final noise as it were.

Well, yes, there is the bang and whimper thing
but now that we know that's out there
I doubt that things will go that way.

It seems like there should already be a reality show
about it being cooked up: "The Final Word."
This implies, of course, we have all agreed
when that final word would take place.

After that point we would all have to stop talking.
That's it then. No more whispering, insulting,
guffawing, flattering, or just general going-on.

No more talks at the beauty parlor or barber shop.
No chatting up somebody while you wait at the car wash.
No shouting to each other at the too-loud bar.

This means songs with words stop, of course.
Most movies, tv shows, news channels.
Telephone calls would be useless.

We could all just stand there and wave our arms
like a bunch of ridiculous mimes,
trying to convey spreadsheets
or the subtle nuances of PTA meetings.

Grunting, whistling, clapping rhythmically,
or humming in tones
would be frowned upon as cheats.

But since I have already written these down
then, of course, it can't be any of these either
or else we could prepare for them.

No. I think it will be something similar to,
but not exactly like, last night,
when I had forgotten something or other
and you had uttered one word
that somehow referenced both me and my lineage,

then you had crawled into bed,
your face to the wall,
leaving me speechless with
your bare back and its apocalyptic indifference.

Prerequisite

Let None But Geometers Enter Here
—motto inscribed above the door at Plato's Academy
where the principal studies were forms and the universe.
4th Century—just outside of Athens.

One would assume you needed to show up
with your own measuring rope.

Or at the very least some pre-defined rod
that was exactly the length from elbow to fingertips.

And a bag-full of pre-conceived notions.
Back then there was no shortage of pre-conceived notions.

Evidently, they wrote endlessly about the stars—
but never went outside to actually study them.

What is the sense of that?
But that's a foolish question

as I sit here, now, in this incredibly uncomfortable chair,
in this equivalent of a suburban, informal academy,

listening to open-mic poets
reading their own poetic philosophies,

and it is obvious they have never stepped outside
themselves to see other constellations.

There should have been a sign
over the doorway into the bookstore.

These poets have not yet learned how to measure.
They should have brought their own rope.

Ultimately

Linnaeus believed in the Grand Design.
In his system there was no mechanism of change
because God designed all organisms perfectly the first time.
—The Day The Universe Changed, James Burke

Having spent the last twenty minutes
trying to untangle the conical wire tomato cages
and realizing in a taxonomic, evolving kind of way
they are related to coat hangers,

I sit here now on a hot metal lounge chair on the patio
sipping a beer and realizing with no little pride
that I fought the many-spindly-legged beast
to a standstill.

It is at moments like this, sweaty and slightly inebriated,
my brain swerves towards phrases and metaphors.
Linnaeus, straight man that he was,
 wouldn't have liked the word swerve.

Perhaps I would mention to him the taunting squirrels
who have not learned their place in this grand scheme.
Or the lizard who has learned to visit my front door to remind me
if I don't sweep the dead bugs he will take care of it.

That might not be enough to set Linnaeus spinning.
So I will mention that evidently God did not design
the wear and tear clause in my lease. Nor did the Almighty
have a finger on the depreciation of my car.

And I suspect it wasn't him who made me buy
the magic rotisserie-oven off late-night t.v.
that broke ten minutes after I got it out of the box.
Linnaeus—I am not done.

God is also probably not the mind behind
"new and improved stickers." Granted, He might be the one
who has helped me be content with the piles of laundry I accumulate—
the whole reverting to a natural state thing—but probably not.

Yet, Linnaeus, I still believe that everything has its place.
Currently, my butt belongs in this hot lawn chair.
And this beer belongs in my hand.
The tangled snarl of tomato cages belongs
on the other side of the yard.

There's an order here, a balance—
my own personal Versailles.
And even so, when the squirrels dig holes willy-nilly,
and the tomatoes die an untethered death,
there will still be more than enough blame to go around.

Recalculating

There is no Royal Road to Geometry.
I could have told Ptolemy that.

Having survived the curriculum-and-ruler-based
Mrs-Zankers-sixth-grade-math-class

I am fairly convinced no cartographer
has ever charted a Royal Road to Geometry.

Having said there is no ROYAL road
the implication is there is a road somewhere

(hidden though it may have been
from clueless and fearful sixth graders.)

I have heard of the Road to Perdition,
The Road to Hell, and the Appian Way.

I have heard of The Mother Road, Abbey Road,
and the Boulevard Saint-Germain.

Those are the easy ones, perfect answers for trivia games.
There are at least a score of others.

I do harbor a certain level of curiosity
about the dress code for these trips,

especially for the Road to Ruin,
and what type of accommodations

one can expect when they get there.
For instance, The Mother Road calls for t-shirts,

and the Road to Hell, or so I imagine at least,
would demand something too glittery or too transparent.

It seems like the Road to Ruin, though, could be a quick trip.
One minute rubies and the next minute rocks.

It would be hard to chart, hard to anticipate,
hard to visualize the rills, canyons, and peaks.

How do you dress for the trip? Do you pack
Ruined Scarves, Ruined Slacks, Ruined Silk Pajamas?

It makes one wonder how to prepare,
makes one visualize the hotel at the other end:

the tiles cracked in the lobby,
glass dropping from the chandeliers,

wallpaper peeling from the walls,
the tub long past redeeming.

You can't even begin to imagine how you ever got here,
how many hours it might take you to get back home.

A Little Conversation about Geometers
at the Center of the Earth

I can certainly imagine the scene where Kepler
or Copernicus or Galileo would want to take
Edgar Rice Burroughs and Jules Verne
and shake the holy cosmological crap out of them
for even suggesting there could be a world
at the center of the earth.

You have to admit—the concept does have a certain
Aristotelian holy spheres beauty to it.
But then there's the centrifugal force
and no-horizon problems to work out.
And gravity would be the least of the issues.

The worst of them would be the lack of stars.

If the scientific excursions had started coming in
from the outer crust,
overburdened with wooden boxes
filled with all types of levels, measuring wheels, and rope,
sextants and astrolabes,
they would have found
a disquieting shifting of faith.
And probably a bunch of Mayans
there ahead of them,
lazing around, drinking pellucidarian expressos.

What use was there in measuring the stars
those confused Europeans would be told!
Why survey the land, count the steps,
carve calendars?
Every day here is a beach day.
The sun is always shining,
There are more than enough other things to discover,
and all things that would conquer us, including Time,
are oh so far away?

Insertion

Sometimes I like to go into the museums
and purposely not insert myself into the paintings.

After all, if Rembrandt had wanted to include me
as one of the Dutch Masters he would have written.

I never got a call from Hopper saying
he had room on a barstool in Nighthawks.

Did Dali ever consider hanging my body limp
and melty over a tree? If he did—he never asked.

Then there were the Babylonians.
They could have carved my effigy onto a lion's body—and didn't.

And those crazy Egyptians have never inquired
about giving me my own cartouche.

I have had to accept their works as complete.
If any of these people walked into the room

and started reading one of my poems
I would not expect him to say, "So, are you done with this? Did you include me?"

I am certainly not on the Wreck of the Medusa
and I am fairly certain I am not blue and playing a guitar.

I was never photographed by Curtis
and I do not think I am referenced in any chapel.

I may have been on a cave painting.
If so, I was the one running away from the bear.

I can imagine myself doing that.
If you go and check I would bet I am still running.

And What Comes Next

Act as if it were impossible to fail
—*Dorothea Brande*

There are mornings of course
when failure is already pre-ordained.
I have heard there is the divining art

that allows certain people to read the swirls
of milk as it pours into coffee.
This morning I swear I acted as if I would

successfully pour the milk into my coffee.
I have done it without failure,
both privately and in public, again and again,

but today, in my bleariness,
when I poured the milk into my coffee
the little swirls made a picture

of what I think was Doris Day
when her hair was pulled up high,
like maybe when she was in a Rock Hudson movie

or in The Pajama Game. And then I had to wonder
why Doris Day would appear to me.
Other people get visitations from dead relatives

or, even better, our Lady of Guadalupe
(although I understand that Lady prefers
the almost gel-fixative qualities of latte foam.)

At least with a dead relative or Lupe
there is a certain amount of expectation
that the visitant has an inside track

about knowledge from the other side
and you really have to bow down to that.
I mean, you just have to.

But with Doris Day I had to ponder
what the rest of the day was going to bring.
Of course I had failed in pouring milk into the coffee

because now I could not stir it,
I could not make little cyclones of Doris Day's face.
It wouldn't have been right.

What other small exquisite failures were awaiting me?
Would the bite of my teeth
into my cheap baked pastry

turn into a perfect scalloping
that would easily line up, curve for curve,
for the shell that ferried Venus?

When I brushed my hair as I was drying it,
something I swear I have done several thousand times
with certainly passing-grade results,

would I somehow end up with a perfect Elvis curl,
as if some spirit was channeled,
and I needed blue suede shoes to get through the day?

Or, finally, as I bent to put on my brown oxfords,
the well-worn ones, who have served me as friends
through puddles and weddings,

yes, those brown oxfords—
would I fail miserably in their tying,
my fingers developing an unexplained, routed, twitch

as they twined the lace into a perfectly artistic,
historically accurate Gordian knot,
designed to make sure

my shoe never left my foot,
no matter how far I walked,
no matter how stiff they looked every night in bed?

Taming And Training Lovebirds

Found at a thrift shop:
Taming and Training Lovebirds
by Risa Teitler, 1988
by T.F.H. Publications, Inc.

After first noticing the happy-looking birds
obviously flirting on the cover,
I then noticed, on the lower corner,
a little sticker telling me the binding was guaranteed for 10 years.
When I bought this book,
it was already over twenty-five years old
so it is safe to say that the cover fulfilled its warranty.

That warranty may or may not come as interesting news
to all the love birds photographed inside.
I would imagine that all of them
had already beaked their last smooch.
several years ago.

When they were still modeling
they appeared as content as wedding couples.
As if yesterday they were simply parrots;
but then the next day they were love birds.
No one can be blamed for liking a more connotative title.
Why, just look at the smitten couple on page seventy-four!
And who could not be moved a little by the pair on page ten?

It makes no difference if they are
Abyssinian lovebirds, black-cheeked lovebirds,
peach-faced, Fischer, black-masked, or Madagascar.
Love is love and even the avian heart can decide.

Still, there is that nagging label.
It is like the slave holding the victory wreath over the conqueror.
These birds might as well be
Julius Caesar or Napoleon.
Or Tsar Nicholas
protecting his family
under a sheltering wing

Or even more
like King Belshazzar
who read the words written on the wall,
and realized there is no plumage
that will not eventually fade,
regardless of how things
seemed to be going so well.

If I Get To Choose

When I shake off this spark that has kept me going
I would ask that you not bury me in a gold coffin.
Or silver. Or platinum. Or, if I have achieved
some level of accomplishment, don't let the town
or province crust me up with rubies or sapphires
or anything like that.
Don't let them fill my tomb with diamond pens
and crystalline quills.

There might be a revolution where my type of poetry
falls horribly out of fashion,
where the populace has to rise up
and deny they ever read anything like my type of poetry,
where the only type of poetry they like
is, well, anything that is totally unlike the Ancient Regime.

Somebody might dig me up, or disinter me,
and take all the precious stuff, and give it to
whoever is reciting now.
And there I'd be, arms crossed, truly a pauper,
staring at nothing, the quietest guy in the room.

Much better to be cremated.
Then I won't be propped up like
some cattle rustler from the wild west.
No one will point at me and take pictures.
No one will post a little sign in front of me that says,
"Here's what happens to people
who weave words the old way.
Those were all his weapons.
You can have any of them you want."

A Different Wild

She told me that a bear had visited her cabin
and she had watched him as he lumbered past,

thick with musk, rolling black head attached to
a corded muscle that joined to the fat-heavy shoulders,

and she knew that the cabin, that the mountain,
would protect her, if she let things have their way.

So the moment passed and she was in the circle
and part of the circle now and maybe there are stories

of angels who have wrestled bears. Or maybe not.
We all measure time different.

I can't keep a watch running on my wrist.
I smash it into things, break the crystal,

the hands give up and fall off. It makes things easier.
I have thought about waking up in a morning

there in my own cabin, no watch on my wrist,
and all I would need for reassurance

to know that I had reached my horizon
would be to see a perfect bear footprint outside my door.

And I would know he had not felt the need to come in and claim me.
He measured time differently.

That would be the gift he could give me,
the best clock I could know.

Belief

Sleeping with the light off is one of the things
I should be better at. I should be better
by now at a lot of things. Filing papers.
Cooking rice. Forming opinions about God.
Not being able to articulate why
red-headed women mean so little to me.
I should be better at so much of this. Life
is linear, like a string, or a long piece
of wood, and everything we do is just a
scratch on it. So does it matter that I don't
know the name of the little white flowers in
my yard? That's a question. I seem to have more
questions. Is this what getting old is? I should
be better at this. I should be better at
loving someone. I should be better walking
through the dark. Last night someone I trust took me
by the hand and led me outside. Along the
telescope of her arm she showed me Venus
shining bright, hanging like a promise. And she
told me some of the other stars. She knew lots
of them. This is one of the things I should be
better at by now I said. I should trust. You
will get better she said. I should be better
at loving you. You have a faith deeper than
mine. She looked at me and smiled and said Venus
will be back tomorrow. Now, let's go cook some
rice. I will show you your faith, my faith. I will
show you, in the dark, what you are still good at.

Risk

I tell everyone else to take risks
but I prefer to hide behind my in-the-moment words.
I have always had a problem
with poets who confess what they are feeling.

Especially considering the fact that
I believe each poem is a contract
where the poet has to convince the reader
the poem belongs to both of them.

Well, that's love then, isn't it?
some of my romantic friends say,
which prompts them into nuzzling in public
which can get ugly really quickly.
It's like writing poetry. You have to
know when to stop.

See what I did there? I diverted,
turned it into a moment again.
But everything is a series of moments.
It's all because we're self-aware.
We think every space we walk through
we instantly make important.

Confession was good enough for St. Augustine
so I should be willing to accept it
from other less talented (and less saint-like) poets.

It's a risk this laying oneself open.
Years ago my father took two old truck hoods
and welded them together.
Then on one end, for a seat,
he bolted a plywood plank
onto a caged, empty, twenty-gallon can.

It was the ugliest boat ever
but it could not be turned over
and all he wanted to do was fish
on a quiet river. That's all.

There's another hobby that's in the moment:
Fishing. It always depends on the x, y, and z
of intersecting time, fish, and bait.
We always hope the fish are waiting for us.
We want to enter into a contract.

Again I have side-stepped. Years ago,
in a moment of what I thought was foresight,
I learned to dance. As it turns out—it is not a skill
like riding a bicycle. You can forget.

But fishing, writing, confessing, dancing—
It's all taking a risk.
You have to be shown how
even if you don't know the name for it
or all the mechanics.

Like my father.
He would walk down the path to the river
and throw the cooler and rods
and bait and net and oar into the boat
Then he would unlock it from its chain
and step in.
He would use the oar to push off from the bank
and he would back up
and sit down on that little square platform.
A smile would cross his face.
He would take a deep breath,
then he would paddle away,
and it was obvious he felt
positively buoyant.

Veritas

Truth Lies in the Bottom of Wells
—Old Greek Proverb

If you read most how-to-write books
almost all of them will tell you to keep a journal.
What they do not say is that it should be pink,
with a tiny little lock, (with a bendy little key),
and there should be a poodle on the cover
with sequins for a collar.
Or maybe that is a diary. Besides, no writer
I know actually writes in a journal. They just tell everyone else
to do it. They may have several blank journals,
pages they definitely intend to fill up later.
If you ask them they will swear to it.

Maybe the old Greeks should have said
that truth lies in the bottom of sock drawers,
the lint trap on the dryer,
the tackle box you never cleaned out
(with dried worms on rusty hooks.)
Remember: you voluntarily bought that exercise machine.
Do you remember where you put the instruction manual?
That place would be overflowing
with the untapped sweat of truth.

It's a catalog—all the places truth could be hiding.
Like one day your kids will find the old photos of you,
pre-braces, with the bad haircut, and the plaid shorts,
and they will wonder what else they don't know.
And you'll laugh with them—but after they leave
you'll bury that box a little deeper.

And you'll start thinking about
where you have put other pieces.
And you'll say "thank god I never wrote in a journal,"
but truth is already ahead of you,
sifting dust in the attic,
reading your old love letters.
Or maybe truth is finding and leaving out on the table
that library book from high school
you always intended to return.

You start finding some mornings
are thinner and less secure than others.
Sometimes, like your own mother,
you will take your coffee black.
Sometimes you will almost swear
there was a message in that darkness.

And sometimes you will worry,
laugh, but still worry,
that a tiny skull will bob to the surface,
its jaws spreading open
ready to speak your name.

The Most Mysterious Thing in the World

What, in any event, is the nature of this "force" that so persistently tugs at the pencil...
—Page 15, The Book of Marvels, copyright 1931

I can honestly say that that force
is probably too much caffeine.
Or maybe the motivation of seeing a beautiful woman.
Or drinking a really good dark beer.

It's only my opinion. This book, though, says
the mysterious force is Gravity.
That explains everything and nothing.
Which is what the best mysterious forces do.

There are lesser mysterious forces—
knowing exactly when to flip a pancake,
understanding when the dog wants out—

but gravity. Yes. That does explain
the leaden feel in my arm, when I was nine,
when I should have been writing
thank you notes to my grandmother.

And I remember I definitely felt it tugging at my pencil
when I wanted to write a love note in the fourth grade
and all I could manage was,
"I had fish sticks for lunch. How about you?"

Gravity makes us all stupid. It trips us.
Puts our face in it. A good dark beer will do that.
But Gravity is free.

I only included the earlier references to beautiful women
and drinking too much coffee
because I consider them both mysterious

but in different ways that are at least
three conversations points away
from what gravity is really good at.

Still, I can honestly say, that in 1931,
I find it very soothing that someone had already discovered
that gravity can push a pencil.

It was somehow reassuring
that they still mentioned pencils,
even as late as 1931,

when ink had certainly been around awhile.
And typesetting. And coffee.
And hormonal urges.

But here, you scholars, who are like me,
who pursue old books—
there must be other Books of Marvels.

Maybe you will find something done by a monk
who had been sitting in a lonesome carrel,
his mind full of all things that bless and curse us,

and you will find an illustration from a illuminated manuscript
where in the unused margin there is a picture of me,
or someone who looks suspiciously like me,

who is chasing some well-endowed, wimpled beauty.
And in one hand I have a nubbed pencil.
And in the other an eternally steaming cup

full of a liquid from a crushed bean.
And I am forever stumbling forward
with a certain intoxicated grin.
And I am very happy with the falling.

In Case of Poetry Reading Break Glass

It is almost certain this is a scenario that will never happen.
If someone spontaneously combusts while reading something by Bukowski then
perhaps they should be allowed to burn. Then let's all go for the axe.

Of course, the sign could read, "In case of fire break glass"
and inside the tiny little alcove, the shelf
barely big enough to hold an ancient dwarf mummy,
would be a poetry book

which most of us, I fear, would not know how to use.
We would stare blankly at it for several seconds,
wondering what possible good it could do us,
how it might yet save our lives.

Voice-Over

There, on the documentary,
how comical the lion looked.

Almost like a cartoon,
when she sat down
and hung onto the gazelle with one paw.

With the other paw I imagined her
scratching behind her ear,
or checking her nails,
or drinking a glass of wine,
or reading Variety.

The narrator of the documentary said
that if the gazelle could once free herself
from that hindering paw
then her speed would let her completely escape.

That all depended, of course,
my argumentative mind said,
on the lion suddenly deciding
to wave with both paws at a best-friend girlfriend lion
just there across the veldt.
Or maybe she would be humming an old catchy tune
and decided impulsively to clap along.

The narration had the artifice of a sporting event
where there is a voice pumping up
our anticipation of a perfect putt for instance,
with something anecdotal added about the ease of stroke
and practiced eye.

Only in the movies is there a voice-over
for the fumbled intricacies of a first kiss
or for a description of the particular angle
of an open elbow that powers the whiskey
pouring down a throat.

I am not sure that a narrator
could add much drama to the tableau of
the rabbit that sneaks into my yard at night
to eat my lettuce.
And I am not even sure that sonorous tones
could augment the emotional landscape

of the shadowy murder of crows
that descends into the grocery store parking lot
for no apparent reason other than group discussion.

And I truly do not anticipate
that several years from now,
or maybe next week,
there will be a camera crew
and a gravelly whispering observer somewhere close by
when I wander far off track
and find myself in the situation
where Death has a hold of my belt in one hand
and with the other hand
he tries unsuccessfully
to stifle a yawn.

Playing Lorca's Piano

Sometimes it is all about the places
we will never see.

Most of us will never sit in Gandhi's cell,
never sleep where Ben Franklin slept.

Stopping at all the historical markers
in all the world would be a lifetime of
Dad turning on the blinker and making sure
there was enough gravel to pull over onto the shoulder.

It might be like wearing Shakespeare's favorite shirt.
You know the one. Foofy shoulders, lace around the wrists.
It's hanging right there in a closet—if you know the right closet.

Or drinking from Dylan Thomas' favorite whiskey glass.
Did you know Coleridge had a stuffed albatross up on a shelf?

In Florida the cats have extra toes.
They are poly-dactyl. We like it because it sounds poetic.
Why do we go there to see?
We like to see visit giant balls of twine,
get tangled in the sight of the Barbed Wire Museum.

"O'Keeffe sat here, in this very chair. Or maybe that chair.
It depended."
So we sit there too. In both. Trying them out.
Thinking we too can admire the light.

Or we sit on the bench in front of Lorca's piano.
And we stroke the keys and we wonder if maybe
some motes are still drifting over the wires,
or there are lingering vibrations we aren't meant to understand.

Basic Element

When the Saints would fall asleep in their hammocks,
with the books over their eyes,
their breath would bless every page.

As if breath could do that.
It's like the space between the eyes
and the putting of words on the paper—
the distance that can't be measured.

It's almost like what you've done here.
Those saints are gone,
I'm removed,
and you are the only one real now.

You could go lay in a hammock and take a nap,
this book over your eyes.

You could fall asleep on the sofa;
this book would fall on your chest, feeling your heartbeat.

Or you could put it on the bed-stand, beside you, at night,
within reach.
(Please leave the light on. It would like that.)

Any way you choose, the words are yours now.
You have breathed them, formed them, warmed them.
Time for you to pass them on. These elements of air.

Euclid knew it all along.
Put it all on paper.
Step aside.

Become invisible.
Then let your lines
prove themselves.

Metamorphoses

Transforming things is where I say:
when Adam and Eve had to leave The Garden
they were given a bag full of parting gifts.

Transforming things is where I say
it's important to remember
that we read in words and phrases
but build a letter at a time.
We watch and listen and disassemble and re-assemble.

Transforming things is where I say
that chiromancy is a wonderful science
that has no basis in science,
which is like saying poetry
has no basis in poetry.
Which is absolutely true.

Poetry is a prime number.
It isn't like anything else.
It's its own story. A story that was seen.
And disassembled. And re-assembled.

Each poem has a life line, a love line, a fate line.

Look. Its little hand is waving you goodbye.

About the Author

Alan Birkelbach was the 2005 Poet Laureate of Texas. His work has appeared in journals and anthologies such as *Grasslands Review, Borderlands, The Langdon Review*, and *Concho River Review*. He has received a Fellowship Grant from the Writer's League of Texas, been named as one of the Distinguished Poets of Dallas, was nominated for a Wrangler, Spur, and Pushcart Prizes, and is a member of both the Texas Institute of Letters and The Academy of American Poets. He has nine collections of poetry.

Acknowledgements

Concho River Review: Prerequisite

Cooking with the Texas Poets Laureate (Texas Review Press): All That Wine Is, Belief

Ilya's Honey: Atlas on His Day Off, Direct Address, Self-Determination

Permian Basin Beyond 2014: Permian Basic Poetry Society: Famous Movie Star, In Case of Poetry Reading Break Glass

Red River Review and *A Texas Garden of Verses:* Vigil

Red River Review: In Praise, The Veritable Speed of Light

River Poets Journal: Metamorphoses

Wichita Falls Literature and Art Review (WFLAR): Leaving Pudd'nhead Wilson, Memento Mori, Semi-Colon, Ultimately

CPSIA information can be obtained
at www.ICGtesting.com
Printed in the USA
FSOW03n2344110515
6994FS